ZIONSVILLE PUBLIC LIBRARY

3 3946 00246 4209

W9-BRT-018

COUNTRY EXPLORERS

RUSSIA

Tom Streissguth

Lerner Publications Company • Minneapolis

Hussey-Mayfield Memorial
Public Library
Zionsville, IN 46077

Copyright © 2008 by Lerner Publishing Group, Inc.

All rights reserved. International copyright secured. No part of this book may be reproduced, stored in a retrieval system, or transmitted in any form or by any means—electronic, mechanical, photocopying, recording, or otherwise—without the prior written permission of Lerner Publishing Group, Inc., except for the inclusion of brief quotations in an acknowledged review.

Lerner Publications Company
A division of Lerner Publishing Group, Inc.
241 First Avenue North
Minneapolis, MN 55401 U.S.A.

Website address: www.lernerbooks.com

Library of Congress Cataloging-in-Publication Data

Streissguth, Thomas, 1958–
    Russia / Tom Steissguth.
      p. cm. — (Country explorers)
    Includes index.
    ISBN-13: 978–0–8225–8664–7 (lib. bdg. : alk. paper)
    1. Russia (Federation)—Juvenile literature. I. Title.
DK510.23.S743 2008
947—dc22   2007019771

Manufactured in the United States of America
1 2 3 4 5 6 – PA – 13 12 11 10 09 08

Table of Contents

Welcome!

We're going to Russia! Russia is easy to find on a map. Some people say it is shaped like a bear. But if you cannot find a bear, just look for the biggest country.

Russia is so large that it is part of two continents— Asia and Europe. The part of Russia that lies in Asia is called Asian Russia. The part of Russia that lies in Europe is called European Russia. The Ural Mountains divide the two parts.

The Ural Mountains run between Asian Russia and European Russia.

4

ASIAN RUSSIA

CENTRAL
SIBERIAN
PLATEAU

EAST
SIBERIAN
UPLANDS

YENISEY RIVER

OB RIVER

IRTYSH RIVER

RUSSIA

WEST
SIBERIAN
PLAIN

S   I   B   E   R   I   A

LENA RIVER

AMUR RIVER

LAKE
BAIKAL

KAZAKHSTAN

MONGOLIA

NORTH
KOREA

JAPAN

SEA
OF
JAPAN

CHINA

PACIFIC
OCEAN

Russia

▲	taiga
	steppes
	tundra
▲	mountains
	desert
★	country's capital

MILES
0   200   400   600

0   400   800
KILOMETERS

5

Siberia

Siberia is the biggest part of Russia. The far northern part of Siberia is called the tundra. In the tundra, the ground below the surface is always frozen.

Snow and ice blanket northern Siberia. Siberia is part of Asian Russia.

South of the tundra is the taiga. The taiga is a huge green forest. It is the largest forest in the world!

Map Whiz Quiz

Take a look at the map on pages 4 and 5. A map is a drawing or chart of a place. Trace the outline of Russia onto a sheet of paper. See if you can find the Baltic Sea. Mark this side of your map with a *W* for west. How about the Pacific Ocean? Mark this side with an *E* for east. Circle the regions labeled European Russia and Asian Russia.

Trees cover the taiga for as far as the eye can see.

Steppe Outside

Russia has many trees and mountains. It also has wide open fields. These fields are known as steppes.

Horses graze in the steppe in southwestern Russia.

Purple wildflowers thrive in this steppe.

The steppes are not like the ones you walk up and down. In fact, they are just the opposite. These grassy fields are so flat that you can see for miles around.

Splash!

Russia has a lot of land—and a lot of water too. Lake Baikal is in southern Siberia. It is the world's deepest lake. The Caspian Sea borders southwestern Russia. It is the largest sea surrounded by land.

The Sayan Mountains reflect off Lake Baikal.

The Volga River starts in northern Russia. It rushes past wheat fields and bustling cities. Then the Volga runs into the Caspian Sea. The Volga is Europe's longest river.

Brainteaser

The Lena River is even longer than the Volga. The Lena is the longest river in Russia. So how can the Volga be the longest river in Europe? Remember that part of Russia is in Europe and part is in Asia. The Lena River runs through Asian Russia.

Russians have a nickname for the Volga River. They call it Mother Volga.

11

On the Move

Subways carry people through the Russian city of Moscow. Subways are trains that run in tunnels underground. They take busy travelers from place to place. Some Russians get around by car. Moscow's streets are full of traffic. Drivers sit in giant traffic jams every day.

Moscow is known for its beautiful subway stations. Chandeliers decorate the ceiling of this station.

Dear Nana,
Mom and Dad took me on a long, long train ride. We even slept on the train. We mostly saw grass from the windows. We met some Russians on the train. All I could say in Russian was hello! I taught one Russian girl how to say hello in English. When we got to the end of the trip, Dad said we were near the Sea of Japan. He says Japan is not far away.

Love,
Maddy

Nana

Your Town

Anywhere US.

ALL ABOARD!

13

People

Many different ethnic groups live in Russia. The people of an ethnic group share a language, a religion, and a history.

These boys are from the Tuva Republic.

Russians are the country's largest ethnic group. They are related to people called Slavs. Slavs lived in the region thousands of years ago. Other ethnic groups in Russia are the Tatars, the Ukrainians, and the Bashkirs.

15

Most people in Russia are ethnic Russians—just like this giggling group of kindergarteners.

Home

Most Russians make their homes in cities. Moscow is Russia's biggest city. It is also the country's capital. Many people in Moscow live in tall apartment buildings.

If you lived in Moscow, you'd probably make your home in a large apartment building.

Russians who live in the country often farm for a living. They might live in simple homes made of wood. Russian farmers grow wheat, potatoes, and other crops.

This wooden cottage sits on Russia's Sakhalin Island.

New Nation

Leaders called czars ruled Russia for hundreds of years. Then, in 1917, some Russians made the czar leave his palace. These Russians formed a new nation. They called it the Soviet Union. The Soviet Union was made up of Russia and many nearby countries.

A statue of Soviet leader Vladimir Lenin stands in Saint Petersburg, Russia.

In 1991, the Soviet Union fell apart. Russia was on its own again. Life in Russia changed. The people got more freedom. But many Russians struggled to find jobs and buy food.

Mikhail Gorbachev

Mikhail Gorbachev led the Soviet Union from 1985 to 1991. He tried to improve the country's government. He wanted to give his people more freedom. People liked his ideas. They wanted to be free. But soon, people wanted more liberty than their government could give them. The Soviet Union began to come apart.

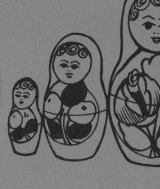

Mikhail Gorbachev speaks at a news conference in October 1985.

Jobs

Many Russians work five days a week. In Russia's cities, workers might have factory jobs. They might make steel, cars, or chemicals. Other workers might have office jobs.

This woman works in a *matryoshka* factory near Moscow. Matryoshkas are Russian nesting dolls.

Some Russians start businesses of their own. This is easier to do these days because Russians have more freedom than they used to.

It is easier to do business in Russia since the Soviet Union broke apart.

Family

In many Russian families, both parents have jobs. Children's grandparents might take care of them while their mom and dad are at work.

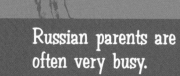

Russian parents are often very busy.

Family Words

Here are the Russian words for family members.

father	atyets	(ah-TYETS)
mother	mat'	(MAHT)
uncle	dyadya	(DZYAH-dzyah)
aunt	tyotya	(TZYOH-tzyah)
grandfather	dyedushka	(DZYAH-doosh-kah)
grandmother	babushka	(bah-BOOSH-kah)
son	sin	(SEHN)
daughter	doch'	(DOYCH)
brother	brat	(BRAHT)
sister	syestra	(seh-STRAH)

Grandmothers are especially important in Russian families. They help with shopping, cooking, and other chores. Russian grandmas are called babushkas.

Food

Russians love good food. Borscht is a popular dinnertime soup. It is bright red! That's because it's made with beets.

Borscht can be served hot or cold. Russians often add sour cream to the soup to give it extra flavor.

Beef Stroganoff is another favorite dish. Beef Stroganoff is a combination of beef stew and noodles. Russians might end a meal with *kompot*. Kompot is a sweet fruit drink.

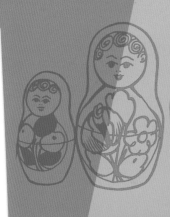

Beef Stroganoff makes a warm, hearty meal.

ABCs

The Russian alphabet is called Cyrillic. It is very different from the alphabet used for English. Only Russian and a few other languages use it.

This Coca-Cola advertisement is written in Cyrillic

If you meet a Russian . . .

here are some good words to know.

yes	da	(DAH)
no	nyet	(NYET)
hello	zdrastvuytie	(ZDRAH-stvwee-tyeh)
good-bye	do svidanniya	(dah-svee-DAHN-yah)

A man named Cyril is said to have invented the Cyrillic alphabet. Cyril lived about one thousand years ago.

A Cyrillic sign hangs outside a restaurant in Moscow. You can probably guess what this sign says!

Holidays

Russians observe many holidays. Some of them have to do with religion. Most people in Russia are Russian Orthodox Christian, Muslim, or Jewish. Each group honors different events.

A Russian Jewish boy makes a craft to honor his religious faith.

Easter is the most important holiday in the Russian Orthodox faith. Families go to church on the night before Easter. They celebrate the day with big feasts. Muslims pray a lot during the month of Ramadan. They also fast from morning until the sun sets. That means they do not eat. On Yom Kippur, Jews pray for forgiveness of their sins.

A Russian Orthodox priest uses holy water to bless Easter cakes and colored eggs.

School

Almost all kids in Russia go to school. Most students attend public schools. Russia's public schools are free.

Elementary school students complete assignments at a school in a Russian village.

Russian children study reading, math, and science. They learn about history and geography too. Does that sound like what you learn about in school?

This smiling student is from Saint Petersburg.

Story Time

Russian children love stories. One well-known story is about a witch. Her name is Baba Yaga. Baba Yaga kidnaps and cooks children. Russian parents warn their children to be good so Baba Yaga doesn't get them.

This picture shows the witch Baba Yaga riding on her broomstick.

Some Russian stories are told through music. *Peter and the Wolf* uses musical instruments to tell a story. Each instrument in *Peter and the Wolf* stands for a different character.

Russia is home to many talented classical musicians.

Some of the world's most famous ballet dancers come from Russia.

Ballet

Many skilled ballet dancers are Russian. They often dance in famous Russian ballets.

34

Swan Lake is one popular ballet.
The Nutcracker is very famous too.
The Nutcracker is a Christmas story.

Russian dancers perform *The Nutcracker* every year at Christmastime.

A Christmas Favorite

A composer named Pyotr Tchaikovsky wrote the music for *The Nutcracker*. This ballet has become a Christmastime favorite. Here is the story:

At Christmas, a girl named Clara receives a wooden nutcracker. The nutcracker looks like a soldier. Later, when Clara goes to bed, she dreams that she is watching a battle take place between her toy soldiers and some mice. Her nutcracker fights the mouse king but must be rescued by Clara. Clara throws her shoe at the king. After the battle, the nutcracker changes into a handsome prince. He leads Clara through the Land of Snowflakes to the Kingdom of Sweets. The kingdom's people dance for the girl. At the end of the ballet, Clara wakes up from her dream.

Music

Music is important to Russians. Lots of talented classical composers have come from Russia. Russians also enjoy folk songs. They love to sing these songs at family gatherings.

These Russian folk musicians are dressed in traditional clothing.

Russia's young people often listen to pop music. They like much of the same music as kids in the United States.

A young woman buys tickets for a concert in Moscow.

Russian ice skaters Tatiana Totmianina and Maxim Marinin won a gold medal at the 2006 Olympic Games in Turin, Italy.

Sports and Fun

Russians often win at worldwide sporting events. Russian athletes train hard. Most of their days are spent practicing.

Soccer is a favorite sport in Russia. A team called the Moscow Spartak plays soccer against teams throughout Europe.

Checkmate!

In school, Russian children learn about czars and czarinas (the wives of czars). But in their time off, kids study kings and queens. These are playing pieces in the game of chess. People play chess in parks throughout Russia. Thousands of Russian children are experts at the game. The world chess champion is almost always a Russian.

Two Spartak players keep their eyes on the ball at a soccer match in Moscow.

New Words

The Russian language looks tricky to many Americans. But you may recognize a word or two in Russian. That's because some Russian words are borrowed from English.

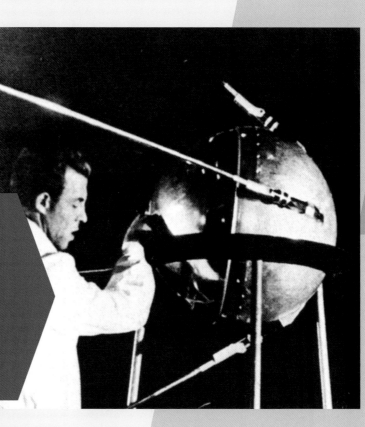

Have you ever heard the word *Sputnik*? *Sputnik* is a Russian word that many Americans know. It's the name for a Russian satellite. The Russians sent the satellite *Sputnik I (right)* into space on October 4, 1957.

The word *biznesmen* is one example. This Russian word means "businessmen." *Jinzi* is the Russian word for jeans. And sneakers in Russia are called *kedi*. This word comes from the brand name Keds.

Do you see any jinzi on this busy Moscow sidewalk?

> Moscow's TV tower reaches high into the sky. The tower allows people to tune in to TV programs.

TV

Television is popular in Russia. Viewers can watch news programs, game shows, movies, and sports.

Young children enjoy *Ulitsa Sezam*—the Russian version
of *Sesame Street*. Zeliboba is a character on *Ulitsa Sezam*.
He is a blue, furry puppet.

A Russian woman watches a news show on the life of Boris Yeltsin. Boris Yeltsin was a former president of Russia.

THE FLAG OF RUSSIA

Russia's flag is white, blue, and red. People have different ideas about what the colors stand for. Some say the white stripe stands for God. Others think it stands for goodness or generosity. Many think the blue stripe represents the czar. It also might stand for honesty and loyalty. The red stripe might represent Russia's people. It may also stand for courage and love.

FAST FACTS

FULL COUNTRY NAME: Russian Federation

AREA: 6.6 million square miles (17.1 million square kilometers), or about twice the size of the United States

MAIN LANDFORMS: the mountain ranges the Urals and the Caucasus; the plateau Central Siberian Plateau; the flatland the West Siberian Plain; the mountains of the East Siberian Uplands

MAJOR RIVERS: Volga, Lena, Don, Ob, Yenisey, Irtysh, Amur

ANIMALS AND THEIR HABITATS: brown bears (forest), Amur leopards (forest), wolves (forest), deer (forest), polar bears (tundra), foxes (tundra), reindeer (tundra), snakes (desert), lizards (desert), antelope (desert)

CAPITAL CITY: Moscow

OFFICIAL LANGUAGE: Russian

POPULATION: about 141,377,752

GLOSSARY

Asian Russia: the part of Russia that lies on the Asian continent

continent: any one of seven large areas of land. The continents are Africa, Antarctica, Asia, Australia, Europe, North America, and South America.

Cyrillic: the Russian alphabet. A few languages besides Russian use this alphabet too.

czar: a Russian ruler. Czars ruled Russia until 1917.

ethnic group: a large community of people that shares the same language, religion, and history

European Russia: the part of Russia that lies on the European continent

map: a drawing or chart of all or part of Earth or the sky

Siberia: the biggest part of Russia. Siberia lies in Asian Russia.

steppe: a wide open field. Steppes cover the southern part of Russia.

subway: a train that runs in a tunnel underground. Subways carry people through the Russian city of Moscow.

taiga: a huge green forest. The taiga stretches from the Gulf of Finland in northwestern Russia to eastern Siberia.

tundra: a region in the far northern part of Siberia. In the tundra, the ground below the surface is always frozen.

TO LEARN MORE

BOOKS

Allman, Barbara. *Dance of the Swan: A Story about Anna Pavlova.* Minneapolis: Millbrook Press, 2001. Anna Pavlova was one of Russia's most famous ballet dancers. This book tells about her interesting life.

Hintz, Martin. *Russia.* New York: Children's Press, 2004. Find out more about the geography, history, and people of Russia in this title.

Zemlicka, Shannon. *Colors of Russia.* Minneapolis: Carolrhoda Books, 2002. From the blue waters of Lake Baikal to the white snow of northeastern Siberia, Russia is a land of many colors. Learn all about Russia's colors in this book.

WEBSITES

A Kid's Life in . . . Russia
http://library.thinkquest.org/CR0212302/russia.html
Read about what life is like for Olia, a ten-year-old girl who lives in Russia.

Russia
http://www.timeforkids.com/TFK/gprussia
This website from the magazine *Time for Kids* features a virtual tour of Russia, a guide to Russian phrases, a quiz about Russia, and more.

INDEX

The photographs in this book are used with the permission of: © Pavel Filatov/Alamy, pp. 4, 9, 14; © age fotostock/SuperStock, pp. 6, 10, 11, 16, 18, 26; © Hubertus Kanus/SuperStock, p. 7; © Jon Arnold Images/SuperStock, p. 8; © Siegfried Layda/Stone/Getty Images, p. 12; © Saverkin Alexander/ITAR-TASS/ CORBIS, p. 13; © vario images GmbH & Co. KG/Alamy, p. 15; © Iain Masterton/Alamy, p. 17; AP Photo/Michel Lipchitz, p. 19; © Shen Bohan/Xinhua Press/ CORBIS, p. 20; AP Photo/Mikhail Metzel, pp. 21, 39; © croftsphoto/Alamy, p. 22; © Bryan & Cherry Alexander Photography, p. 23; © Stock Food Creative/Getty Images, p. 24; © Lew Robertson/ Stock Food Creative/Getty Images, p. 25; © transit/Peter Arnold, Inc., p. 27; © Yuri Tutov/AFP/Getty Images, pp. 28; © Alexander Nemenov/AFP/Getty Images, p. 29; © Heldur Netocny/Panos Pictures, p. 30; © SuperStock, Inc./SuperStock, p. 31; © Mary Evans Picture Library/Alamy, p. 32; © Peter Titmuss/Alamy, p. 33; AP Photo/Alexander Zemlianichenko, p. 34; © Sergio Perez/Reuters/CORBIS, p. 35; © Buddy Mays/TRAVEL STOCK, p. 36; © Natalia Kolesnikova/AFP/Getty Images, p. 37; AP Photo/Itsuo Inouye, p. 38; NASA, p. 40; © Picpics/Alamy, p. 41; © Seamas Culligan/ZUMA Press, p. 42; © Anatoly Maltsev/epa/CORBIS, p. 43.
Illustrations by © Bill Hauser/Independent Picture Service.

Cover: © Janicek/Taxi/Getty Images

11|10